≥ from

orne About the

MAGIC TREE HOUSE® FACT TRACKERS

When I write Magic Tree House® adventures, I love including facts about the times and places Jack and Annie visit. But when readers finish these adventures, I want them to learn even more. So that's why we write a series of nonfiction books that are companions to the fiction titles in the Magic Tree House® series. We call these books Fact Trackers because we love to track the facts! Whether we're researching dinosaurs, pyramids, Pilgrims, sea monsters, or cobras, we're always amazed at how wondrous and surprising the real world is. We want you to experience the same wonder we do—so get out your pencils and notebooks and hit the trail with us. You can be a Magic Tree House® Fact Tracker, too!

Mary Pope Osborne

Here's what kids, parents, and teachers have to say about the Magic Tree House® Fact Trackers:

"They are so good. I can't wait for the next one. All I can say for now is prepare to be amazed!" —Alexander N.

"I have read every Magic Tree House book there is. The [Fact Trackers] are a thrilling way to get more information about the special events in the story." —John R.

"These are fascinating nonfiction books that enhance the magical time-traveling adventures of Jack and Annie. I love these books, especially *American Revolution*. I was learning so much, and I didn't even know it!" —Tori Beth S.

"[They] are an excellent 'behind-the-scenes' look at what the [Magic Tree House fiction] has started in your imagination! You can't buy one without the other; they are such a complement to one another." —Erika N., mom

"Magic Tree House [Fact Trackers] took my children on a journey from Frog Creek, Pennsylvania, to so many significant historical events! The detailed manuals are a remarkable addition to the classic fiction Magic Tree House books we adore!" —Jenny S., mom

"[They] are very useful tools in my classroom, as they allow for students to be part of the planning process. Together, we find facts in the [Fact Trackers] to extend the learning introduced in the fictional companions. Researching and planning classroom activities, such as our class Olympics based on facts found in *Ancient Greece and the Olympics*, help create a genuine love for learning!" —Paula H., teacher

MAGIC TREE HOUSE® FACT TRACKER

Texas

A NONFICTION COMPANION TO MAGIC TREE HOUSE #30:

Hurricane Heroes in Texas

BY MARY POPE OSBORNE
AND NATALIE POPE BOYCE

ILLUSTRATED BY ISIDRE MONÉS

A STEPPING STONE BOOK™

Random House 🏠 New York

The Magic Tree House Fact Tracker series was formerly known as the Magic
Tree House Research Guide series.

Visit us on the Web!
SteppingStonesBooks.com
MagicTreeHouse.com

Educators and librarians, for a variety of teaching tools, visit us at
RHTeachersLibrarians.com

Library of Congress Cataloging-in-Publication Data
Names: Osborne, Mary Pope, author. | Boyce, Natalie Pope, author. | Mones,
Isidre, illustrator.
Title: Texas : a nonfiction companion to Magic Tree House #30: Hurricane
heroes in Texas / Mary Pope Osborne, Natalie Pope Boyce ; illustrated
by Isidre Mones.
Description: New York : Random House Books for Young Readers, 2018. |
Series: Magic Tree House Fact Tracker ; 39 | Includes bibliographical references
and index.
Identifiers: LCCN 2017054538 (print) | LCCN 2018007705 (ebook) |
ISBN 978-1-101-93650-4 (ebook) | ISBN 978-1-101-93648-1 (paperback) |
ISBN 978-1-101-93649-8 (lib. bdg.)
Subjects: LCSH: Texas—History—Juvenile literature. | BISAC: JUVENILE
NONFICTION / History / United States / State & Local. | JUVENILE
NONFICTION / Readers / Chapter Books. | JUVENILE NONFICTION /
People & Places / United States / General.
Classification: LCC F386.3 (ebook) | LCC F386.3.O83 2018 (print) |
DDC 976.4—dc23

Printed in the United States of America

10 9 8 7 6 5 4 3 2 1

This book has been officially leveled by using the F&P Text Level Gradient™
Leveling System.

Random House Children's Books supports the First Amendment and celebrates
the right to read.

For Sam Smith and Don Temples.
Deep in the heart.

Historical Consultant:
ANDREW J. TORGET, professor of history, University of North Texas

Education Consultant:
HEIDI JOHNSON, language acquisition and science education specialist, Bisbee, Arizona

Special thanks to everyone at Random House: Mallory Loehr, Jenna Lettice, Isidre Monés, Paula Sadler, Jason Zamajtuk, and Diane Landolf, the best editor anywhere

TEXAS

Contents

Dear Readers,

In <u>Hurricane Heroes in Texas</u>, we visited Galveston, Texas, during the hurricane of 1900. In just one night, raging winds and floods almost destroyed the city. Many people died or were injured, and the city lay in ruins. It was the biggest weather disaster in American history.

We read about the courage and spirit shown by Texans after the storm of 1900 and after Hurricane Harvey in 2017. That made us want to track the facts about this amazing state and its people.

We learned that Texas has a rich history. Texas has been part of six nations—it was even its own country! We also found out what Texas is like today. It has some huge cities with tall buildings. And every year, thousands of people visit the Alamo, where Texans fought and died for freedom in 1836. Let's travel to Texas to learn all about this great state!

Jack

Annie

1

Texas

Everything is bigger in Texas! That's what
Texans say, and they might be right. The
state itself is huge. It covers more than
260,000 square miles. Alaska is the largest
state in area, and Texas comes in second.
It's about two times the size of Germany
and bigger than France and England put
together!

Texans brag about a thirty-five-foot-high

statue of cowboy boots and a state capitol building almost fifteen feet higher than the U.S. Capitol Building in Washington, D.C.!

Over the years, Texas has belonged to six different nations. One of those was when it was its own separate country.

Before they became states, Hawaii and Vermont were also separate countries.

Texas has a long history. Spanish explorers sailed from Europe and arrived there in 1519. That is about a hundred years before English people settled in Plymouth, Massachusetts, and Jamestown, Virginia.

Texas Today

Texas is in the southwestern part of the United States. It shares a 2,000-mile border with Mexico and has 367 miles of coastline along the Gulf of Mexico. Oklahoma, New Mexico, Arkansas, and Louisiana are its neighbors.

Because Texas is so huge, the land and climate are different throughout the state. The west is flat with hot, dry deserts and very little rain. People there raise cattle and cotton.

The Gulf Coast has miles of sandy beaches, but it also has a high risk of hurricanes. East Texas is lush and green with large pine forests and fields. It gets enough rain for farmers to grow crops like fruits, nuts, and vegetables.

This grapefruit grove is in South Texas.

Rivers and Mountains

Texas has ninety-one mountain peaks that are over a mile high. The Rio Grande River runs almost 2,000 miles from Colorado down to the Gulf of Mexico and marks the border between Texas and Mexico. It's the fourth-longest river in the United States.

Rio Grande means "big river" in Spanish.

The First Texans

The first people to come to what is now Texas arrived about 15,500 years ago. Their ancestors probably walked over a land bridge joining Asia to Alaska.

In 1982, Texas highway workers uncovered the fossils of a woman who lived between 10,000 and 13,000 years ago.

These early people couldn't write, but we know things about them. They made stone tools and hunted with spears. There are fossils in caves of some of the animals they killed. Many—like mammoths,

Much of the art is beautiful and colorful.

giant ground sloths, dire wolves, and huge buffalo—no longer exist.

We've also learned about them from rocks that they painted or carved. The rocks have pictures of humans, buffalo, mountain lions, deer, and birds. Some rocks have simple handprints as if to say, "Look! I was here!"

Tribes in Texas

When the Spanish came in the 1500s, Native Americans were already living in

18

what is now Texas. These included the Lipan Apache, Karankawa, and Caddo. During the next 300 years, Comanche, Cherokee, Choctaw, and Kickapoo tribes began living there as well.

Each tribe had its own language and way of life. Some moved around, hunting buffalo and other animals. Others lived in villages, where they fished and grew crops.

The name Texas comes from a Caddoan word, taysha (TAY-shaw), which means "friends."

The Caddo lived and farmed in East Texas.

Look What Lived in Texas!

Millions of years ago, amazing animals, including *T. rex*, lived in Texas. They existed before humans were on earth. Here are some you might not know about:

Deinonychus

(dy-NON-ih-kus) lived 110 million years ago. They hunted in packs and had a five-inch claw on their back feet that they probably used to kill prey or defend themselves. *Deinonychus* were about eleven feet long and had about seventy super-sharp teeth!

Torosaurus

(TOR-uh-SAW-rus) had a skull over nine feet long, one of the largest skulls of any animal that has ever lived! *Torosaurus* were around twenty-four

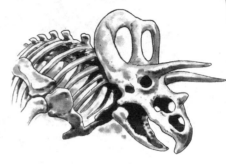

feet long and munched on leaves and other plants. They lived 66 million years ago.

Quetzalcoatlus

(KET-zul-koh-AHT-lus) were not dinosaurs. They were flying reptiles the size of a small airplane! *Quetzalcoatlus* had a huge wingspan that could reach thirty-six feet. Their beaks were up to eight feet long! Yikes!

2

The Spanish Arrive

Spain is a country in Europe. In the 1500s, Spanish explorers, called *conquistadors* (kon-KEES-tuh-dorz), began to explore parts of North and South America. The word *conquistador* means conqueror (KON-kur-er). The conquistadors wanted to take over new lands for Spain. One of their goals was to bring silver, gold, and other riches back to Spain. In the 1500s, conquistadors came to what is now Texas and Mexico.

Exploring Texas

One of the first conquistadors to see Texas was Alonso Álvarez de Pineda. He was an explorer and mapmaker. In 1519, Pineda sailed along the coast of Texas and drew a map of the coastline. It was the first map ever made of Texas. For many years, people used it as their guide.

Cabeza de Vaca

Maybe the most famous conquistador was Álvar Núñez Cabeza de Vaca. In 1528, he was shipwrecked off the coast of Texas. Cabeza de Vaca lived with Native Americans for about six years, part of that time as their slave. But he also worked with the natives as a trader and healer. Cabeza de Vaca admired the way the Native Americans lived and was friends with many of them.

Álvar Núñez Cabeza de Vaca

When he got back to Spain, Cabeza de Vaca wrote a book about his adventures. It was the first book about the geography, wildlife, and native cultures in Texas.

Cabeza de Vaca means "cow's head" in Spanish!

Arrival of the French

Robert de La Salle was a French explorer who made several trips to Canada and the United States. In 1682, La Salle sailed down the Mississippi River from Illinois to the Gulf of Mexico.

France wanted land in North America.

In 1684, the King of France sent La Salle and about 300 settlers to start a French colony, and they landed in southeast Texas. They built a

Robert de La Salle

fort called Fort Saint Louis on the coast.

Many in La Salle's group died from disease or raids by Native Americans. People complained that he was a bad leader. In 1687, some of his men ambushed and killed him. Two years later, Native Americans attacked the fort, killing most of the settlers who remained there.

Missions in Texas

The Spanish called Mexico and its other settlements in the Americas "New Spain."

Texas was part of northern Mexico. Because not many Europeans had settled that northern area, Spain wanted to make it a more important part of New Spain and keep it from the French. It also wanted more control over the native people there. So the Spanish decided to teach the Native Americans to be more like them.

Spain was a Catholic country where everyone spoke Spanish. The Spanish king ordered missions to be built in different parts of what is now Texas. Missions are places where priests live, work, and practice their religious beliefs. Some had schools, hospitals, and farms.

There were a total of twenty-six missions built over a period of about 100 years.

The priests' main goal was to convert, or change, Native Americans into Catholics. They promised them food,

Mission San José in San Antonio is sometimes called Queen of the Missions.

shelter, and protection from attacks by other tribes if they lived with them in the missions.

Daily Life in the Missions

As protection, Spanish soldiers often lived near the missions in forts called presidios.

At the missions, life was strict. There were times when people were supposed to sleep, pray, sing, and work. Priests often treated the natives like slaves.

Native Americans helped to build the missions and planted crops like corn, squash, and beans.

Native people who lived in a mission were not allowed to leave. Many wanted to keep their old customs. They escaped at certain times of the year to fish, trade, and hunt the way they always had. If soldiers managed to track them down,

People at the missions also raised cattle and sheep.

they brought them back and punished them.

The Missions Close

While some of the missions were slightly successful, most were not. Very few natives became Catholics or wanted to live like the Spanish did. Much of the time the natives went to missions only for food or protection and didn't stay very long. By the 1790s, Spain began to close most of its missions.

After 300 years of Spanish rule, the Mexicans began fighting for freedom from Spain. There was a long struggle, and Mexico became a free country in 1821. Texas remained a part of northern Mexico.

Two of the old missions became

Mexican forts with little towns surrounding them. The rest lost their land to settlers who took it for farming and ranching.

What Happened to the Native Americans?

Native Americans suffered at the hands of the explorers and settlers. The newcomers brought diseases like cholera (KAH-luh-ruh) and smallpox, which killed thousands of natives.

During the 1700s and 1800s, settlers—Spanish, Mexican, and American—moved into Texas. They created towns, farms, and ranches. The natives had to fight to keep their lands from being taken over.

Some tribes raided towns and ranches to get things they needed or wanted.

Texans fought back. The Texas-Indian Wars lasted through much of the 1800s.

The settlers and soldiers began pushing Native Americans out of the state.

 Comanche and Apache warriors were daring riders and fierce fighters. The Comanche, known as the Lords of the Plains, were the most powerful and feared tribe.

Quanah Parker, Comanche chief

They destroyed native villages and killed men, women, and children.

By about 1875, the natives had lost several fights, and the Texas-Indian Wars ended. Most of the Native Americans were forced to live in Oklahoma on lands that the government called Indian Territory.

There had once been thousands of Native Americans in Texas. In 1900, only about 470 remained.

Many Comanches had to live near Fort Sill in Oklahoma.

Tejanos

Long before American settlers arrived, Mexicans had ranches and farms in Texas. Today, Mexican Texans are known as *Tejanos* (tay-HA-nohz). This is a Spanish word for "Texans." Tejanos have played an important role in Texas history.

The cultures of Spain and Mexico remain a big part of Texas. Because many Tejanos speak Spanish, there are lots of Spanish signs. Many buildings look Spanish or Mexican. And there are more Mexican restaurants in Texas than in any other state!

Tejano music has strong Mexican roots.

One Popular Tejano music style, Conjunto, features accordion and a Mexican twelve-string guitar.

Omar Garza performed with his high school band, La Tradición, at a festival of Conjunto music.

3

Americans Settle Texas

The Mexicans thought Texas would be a stronger part of their country if more people lived there. In 1821, an American named Stephen F. Austin got permission for 300 American families to settle in Texas. They had to promise they would be loyal to Mexico and swear that they were Catholic.

Settlers began farming and ranching along the Colorado and Brazos Rivers. The

Tejanos welcomed them. They felt that having more people in the region would give Texas more power in the Mexican government.

Other people from the United States who didn't have permission to be in Texas also began arriving. Soon there were more Americans than Tejanos.

The white settlers came to dislike some of the laws that Mexico made them follow. One was a Mexican law against slavery. Many cotton growers came from the American South. Owning slaves had not been against the law there. They depended on their slaves to work for them and didn't want to free them.

There were other reasons that American settlers were unhappy. Most were not actually Catholic and didn't speak Spanish. They had closer ties to the United States than to Mexico. To keep trouble from spreading, in 1830, Mexico ruled that American settlers were no longer welcome in Texas.

Stephen F. Austin Goes to Mexico

Stephen F. Austin went to Mexico in 1833 to meet with President Santa Anna.

Stephen F. Austin

He wanted Texas to become a separate state within Mexico. Santa Anna decided that Austin was a troublemaker and put him in jail for eight months.

Texas Revolution

A revolution happens when people fight to change their government.

Texans didn't want to be controlled by Mexico any longer. They wanted to be a separate country. They wanted a *revolution*! The Texas Revolution began in 1835 when Mexican soldiers went to Gonzales, Texas, to take a small cannon from the people there. The Texans refused to give up the cannon. They taunted the Mexicans by hauling up a flag with a picture of a cannon on it and the words "Come and Take It."

There was a short fight, and two Mexican soldiers were killed. The Mexicans left Gonzales without their cannon.

Remember the Alamo!

The most famous battle in the Texas Revolution was at the Alamo in San

Antonio. The Alamo was an old mission that became a Mexican fort. In December 1835, a small force of armed Texans took over the Alamo.

On February 23, 1836, General Santa Anna, the president

Antonio López de Santa Anna

of Mexico, arrived with more than a thousand troops. He vowed to recapture the Alamo.

William Travis and James Bowie commanded about 200 fighters inside the fort. Travis was a young lawyer and soldier.

William Travis

James Bowie was a skilled knife fighter and soldier.

Among the Texans at the Alamo was Juan Seguín, a Tejano soldier who later became mayor of San Antonio.

James Bowie

Frontiersmen explore or live in wilderness that borders a settled area.

Davy Crockett, a famous bear hunter, soldier, U.S. congressman, and *frontiersman,* also came to fight. He had only been in Texas for three months.

Davy Crockett

Santa Anna's soldiers surrounded the Alamo. The men inside fired down at them over the walls. The two armies fought for thirteen days. Before the end of the standoff, Juan Seguín was sent away to gather more troops.

Juan Seguín

In the early morning of March 6, Santa Anna's army began a fierce attack on the fort. They charged at the wall three times. Finally, it was damaged enough that Santa Anna's soldiers could climb over it. They were inside!

After a bloody fight, all the defenders in the Alamo died, including Bowie, Travis, and Crockett. News of their deaths made Texans more determined than ever to fight for freedom. The Alamo was a symbol of their struggle.

The fight lasted about ninety minutes.

The Fall of the Alamo was painted in 1903.

San Jacinto

Sam Houston was shot in the ankle.

While the battle at the Alamo was going on, General Sam Houston was building his army. A month later, he and his men joined Juan Seguín's Tejano troops to surprise Santa Anna's army at San Jacinto. After a fight lasting only eighteen minutes, the Texans defeated Santa Anna's soldiers. During the fight, the Texans' battle cry was "Remember the Alamo!"

After the defeat of the Mexican army at San Jacinto, Texas became the Republic of Texas.

The *republic*'s flag had only one star. It stood for the country of Texas. People still call Texas the Lone Star State.

The Twenty-Eighth State

Nine years later, Texas joined the United States. Sam Houston thought that being part of the United States would make Texas safer from Mexico. He also told

The president of the Republic of Texas lowered the flag when Texas became a state.

his fellow Texans that being a U.S. state would help their businesses. In 1845, Texas became the twenty-eighth state.

The Civil War

In 1861, *civil war* began between Northern and Southern states. The North wanted the South to free their slaves. The South refused and broke away from the United States to form its own government. They named it the Confederate States of America.

Civil war is a war between people who belong to the same country.

Since Texans owned about 180,000 slaves in 1861, the state joined the Confederate cause.

After four years of the bloodiest fighting in U.S. history, the South lost the war. Texans had to free their slaves and take a vow to be loyal to the

United States. In 1870, Texas became a state again.

Six Flags

Six different flags have flown over Texas, one for each nation that ruled the state. Can you remember what they were?

In case you can't, they were: Spain, France, Mexico, the Republic of Texas, the Confederate States of America, and the United States of America.

Spain

France

Mexico

Republic of Texas

Confederate States of America

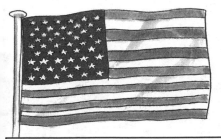

United States of America

4

Great Galveston Hurricane

In 1900, TVs and radios didn't exist. News traveled slowly from one place to another. There were weather stations and weather forecasters, but they didn't have the equipment that we have today. It was very hard to predict the weather.

Galveston was the largest city in Texas. It was also one of the richest in the country. The city was on an island in the Gulf of Mexico that was twenty-seven miles long. Bridges and train tracks connected the island to the mainland.

Galveston had one of the busiest harbors in the country. Almost all the cotton in the country shipped out from its port.

Downtown Galveston was bustling in 1898.

In 1900, 40,000 people lived in the city. Tourists visited its beautiful beaches and admired the elegant houses that lined the streets.

Most hurricanes happen from June to November, when ocean water is warmest. On September 4, 1900, the weather service sent word that a tropical storm that had begun off the coast of Africa had hit Cuba.

Some hurricanes are over 300 miles wide!

Storms turn into hurricanes when their winds are over 74 miles per hour. The winds push the storm thousands of miles across the ocean. When a hurricane passes over warm water, it gets more powerful. Because the earth turns, hurricanes move in a circle.

On the morning of September 7, no one in Galveston was worried about a storm. People didn't know that a massive hurricane was headed their way.

Galveston was only eight feet above sea level. For years, people had talked about building a seawall around the city to protect it from flooding. They decided not to. They even removed sand dunes to give the city more land.

 The hurricane traveled over Cuba and west of Florida before it hit Galveston.

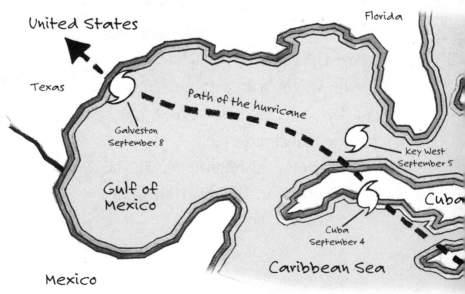

United States

Florida

Texas

Path of the hurricane

Galveston
September 8

Key West
September 5

Gulf of
Mexico

Cuba

Cuba
September 4

Mexico

Caribbean Sea

The Hurricane Hits

On September 8, the hurricane slammed into the city with winds over 140 miles per hour. A fifteen-foot *storm surge* flooded streets and destroyed train tracks and bridges that linked the city to the mainland. Nothing was safe from the awesome power of the storm.

A storm surge happens when strong winds push a huge amount of water on land.

Before telephones, people sent messages by telegram. The messages traveled through electrical lines. Because the wind had blown down all the telegraph poles, there was no way to get news out of the city. Galveston was cut off from the rest of the world.

Terror at Night

As night fell, the wind blew harder, and the water rose higher. Buildings toppled over, and people huddled in terror on roofs as their houses blew out to sea.

Mother Mary Joseph Dallmer

Many people showed amazing courage. Mother Mary Joseph Dallmer was one of them. She was a nun who was head of the Ursuline Academy, a Catholic girls' school.

Ursuline Academy

Mother Mary Joseph had just welcomed her new students for the fall. When the hurricane hit, water rose nine feet on the school's first floor. Mother Mary Joseph told everyone to run to the second floor. As people huddled together, wind blew out the windows.

Mother Mary Joseph stayed calm. She and her nuns stood at the windows with ropes and threw them out to rescue people

from the flood. They rang the big school bell
so survivors could find them in the dark.

Two nuns ran to the kitchen for supplies.
When they didn't return, everyone thought
they'd drowned. But they were found the

next day. They had stayed alive by floating on a big bread tray!

After the storm, the nuns took care of anyone who made it to the Ursuline Academy. They saved more than a thousand people! Mother Mary Joseph was a hero of the Galveston Hurricane.

Three women gave birth to babies at the academy that night.

This high school was one of the many buildings destroyed by the hurricane.

Destruction Everywhere

The hurricane lasted about eight hours. In the morning, people crept out to find their beautiful city was gone. Buildings looked as if a giant had smashed them. Experts think that 6,000 to 12,000 people were dead or missing.

The hurricane destroyed 3,600 houses and most of the buildings in Galveston, including schools, churches, and hospitals.

After the Hurricane

Galveston was in crisis. There was no shelter for anyone. There was no food or water. People didn't have clothes or medicine.

On September 9, a ship from Galveston harbor managed to reach Texas City, a short distance away, carrying news of the disaster. Word spread to the governor of

Texas and the U.S. president. Newspapers all around the country alerted people that Galveston had gone through a terrible disaster.

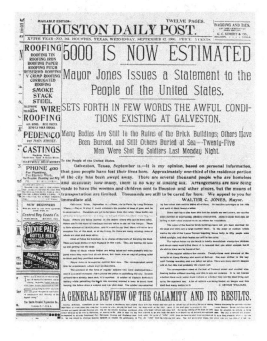

Texans everywhere pitched in to help. Workers from Houston arrived with clean water and food for the 30,000 people who were homeless. A great number of survivors took shelter in white army tents.

There were so many army tents on Galveston Beach that people called it the White City on the Beach.

After the Storm

To keep floods from ever happening again, workers hauled in millions of tons of sand to raise the whole city seventeen feet aboveground. They managed to pack the sand under 2,146 buildings!

They also built a strong seawall. But even though Galveston got back on its feet, it was never again the powerful city it had been before the hurricane.

The Galveston hurricane killed more people than any hurricane in U.S. history. There are many books, movies, and songs about this one unforgettable night in Galveston.

St. Patrick Church weighed over 3,000 tons. It took 700 jacks to lift it up so people could put sand under it.

The Galveston seawall is ten miles long.

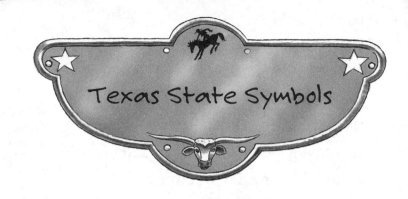

Texas State Symbols

Mammal: Texas Longhorn

Bird: Northern Mockingbird

Flower: Bluebonnet

Dog: Blue Lacy

Horse: American Quarter Horse

Flag: Lone Star

Tree: Pecan

Hat: Cowboy

Insect: Monarch Butterfly

Reptile: Horned Lizard

5

Cattle and Oil

Ranching is part of Texas history. In the 1830s, when Americans began settling in Texas, many of them raised cattle.

At first, ranchers raised longhorn cattle. The Spanish had brought these longhorns with them when they first came to Mexico. Over the years, the cattle wandered into Texas. American ranchers could have as many as they wanted. There were millions of them, and the ranchers could get them for free!

 Longhorns have horns that can measure about six feet across!

Ranchers hired cowboys to work on their ranches. The first cowboys were

Mexicans called *vaqueros* (vah-KARE-oze). Vaqueros had worked on ranches for over 200 years. They had skills that American cowboys did not have yet.

When Americans started ranching in Texas, the vaqueros often taught them how to be cowboys. They showed new ranch hands how to rope, brand, and herd cattle. They also advised them about the clothes, rope, and saddles that they needed.

Today Texas is still the number one state for cattle, cotton, sheep, hay, horses, and goats.

Ranching became a bigger business after the Civil War ended and trains came to more towns. Ranchers were able to ship their cattle to other parts of the country faster. With more beef in the stores, Americans began to eat a lot more meat. From 1860 to 1880, Texas ranchers sold over 10 million cattle.

Modern ranchers often ride ATVs instead of horses.

Richard King, who started the ranch in 1853, came from a very poor Irish family in New York City.

Texans have more cattle than any other state. Ranchers raise different kinds of cattle, not just longhorns. While there are new ranches, some famous old ones are still going strong.

One of the most famous is the King Ranch in South Texas. It dates back to the middle of the 1800s. The ranch covers over 825,000 acres. That's larger than the state of Rhode Island!

These cowboys rounded up cattle on King Ranch in 1950.

Today 400 people work at the ranch. They raise cattle and horses and grow crops. The ranch hasn't forgotten the first cattle that roamed the range there. They still keep two small herds of long-horns.

Black Gold

There is treasure buried deep underground in Texas. It's not diamonds or

gold—it's oil and natural gas. Texans call their oil black gold.

Oil and natural gas come from plants, bacteria, and animals that died millions of years ago. As time passed, they became fossils buried deep in the earth. Layers of dirt and rock pressed down on the fossils and heated them up. Heat and pressure changed the fossils into oil and natural gas.

Because they're from fossils, we call them fossil fuels.

Use Fossil Fuels for Energy:

Stoves
Cars, trucks,
     and other machinery
Furnaces

Spindletop

In the early 1900s, people began to need a lot of oil and gas for their cars and factories. Finding it could be a problem.

Oil is usually about a mile underground. In 1901, Anthony Lucas, an oil explorer, thought there was a lot of oil in Texas. He chose Spindletop Hill, outside of Beaumont, as a perfect spot to drill for it.

Lucas drilled 1,000 feet down. Suddenly, oil gushed out of the drilling hole. Lucas and his men looked on in amazement as an oil spray rose 150 feet in the air!

When oil shoots high up in the air, it's called a gusher.

For nine days, Spindletop pumped about 100,000 gallons of oil a day!

After Spindletop, people discovered oil all around Texas. The state was in the midst of an oil boom. For years, thousands of Texas oil pumps bobbed up and down twenty-four hours a day, pumping oil out of the ground. Many are still going. They look like giant drinking birds.

Texas makes 35 percent of the nation's oil. That's much more than any other state. Almost 200,000 Texans work in the oil business.

The Biggest Blast

On the morning of April 16, 1947, workers were loading fertilizer onto a ship in Texas City harbor. Fertilizer has a chemical in it that explodes when it is packed tight in a container and gets too hot. No one is sure, but it's possible that someone accidentally threw a lit cigarette near the 2,300 tons of fertilizer on board.

A fire started, and later there was a massive explosion. It was so loud that people heard it from 150 miles away! The blast also blew out windows in Houston, 40 miles away.

A mushroom-shaped cloud shot 2,000 feet in the air, and a 15-foot tsunami rolled onto shore. Oil tankers in the harbor caught fire and burned. The water got so hot that it boiled. Fires burned for three days.

Two thousand people lost their homes. As many as 600 people died, and thousands were injured. Only one firefighter in the Texas City fire department survived. It was the biggest explosion in U.S. history.

6

Space City

Since 1961, Houston, Texas, has been home to the Lyndon B. Johnson Space Center. The center is in charge of all manned U.S. space flights, plus the U.S. and international space stations.

Over the years, 500 astronauts have trained at the Johnson Space Center. This includes every U.S. astronaut who has been on a space shuttle.

Astronaut Training at the Center

Teams of scientists at the center have an important job. They must send astronauts 240 miles above the earth at a speed of 17,500 miles per hour! Each mission costs hundreds of millions of dollars.

Because life in space is so different from life on Earth, the astronauts usually train for two years before going up. They often practice on virtual-reality machines that teach them how to operate the space station.

The word **astronaut** comes from the Greek words for "star sailor."

The astronaut Robert L. Crippen floated around on the space shuttle <u>Columbia</u> in 1981.

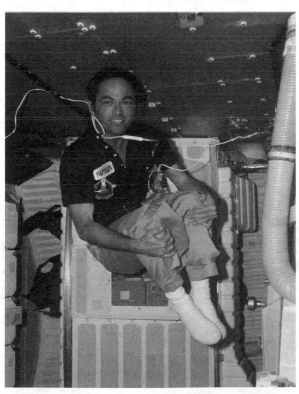

Lack of gravity in space makes their bodies almost weightless. When they're in space, the astronauts float around and move very slowly.

To prepare themselves, they spend time underwater in a swimming pool that is four stories deep! The force of the water teaches them how they'll feel in the space station.

Underwater training

Blast Off!

Astronauts travel to the International Space Station in Russian Soyuz spacecraft. A rocket on each spacecraft propels them into space, where the astronauts then hook up with the space station. Space stations are like laboratories that orbit Earth. The astronauts live there for about six months, doing experiments and research.

Back at mission control, hundreds of people make sure the trip is successful and that the astronauts stay safe. There are people working twenty-four hours a day, seven days a week.

Apollo 13

One of the scariest moments in space travel happened in April 1970. Apollo 13 was on its way to the moon with three astronauts aboard. Suddenly an oxygen tank exploded. The men knew that they were in danger of dying from lack of oxygen.

Apollo 13 crew

Mission control called on experts from all over to work on solving the problem. They canceled the moon landing and focused on saving the astronauts' lives.

With the help of mission control and their own long training, the astronauts managed to splash down in the ocean safely. They were rescued forty-five minutes later. Everyone in mission control cheered!

Astronaut Jack Swigert first alerted the control room about the explosion by saying, "Houston, we've had a problem." Swigert is still famous for his coolness in an emergency. Even today when things go wrong, people say, "Houston, we've had a problem."

Texans at Play

A University of Texas football game is an amazing sight. The team's name is the Texas Longhorns.

- **The Eyes of Texas:** Fans start each game singing "The Eyes of Texas." They sing "Texas Fight!" during the game.
- **Texas Longhorn Band:** The marching band enters the field led by a drummer banging on Big Bertha, the biggest bass drum in the world.

- **Smoky the Cannon ("Old Smoky"):** Someone fires Old Smoky, a cannon like ones that soldiers used in the Civil War.
- **Bevo:** A Texas longhorn that is always named Bevo stands at one end of the field. Since 1916, there have been fifteen Bevos.

- **Slogan:** The fans yell "Hook 'em, Horns!" to show their fighting spirit. They hold up their index and little fingers like horns and wave signs around.
- **Flag:** People unroll a giant Texas state flag on the field. It's 100 feet wide and 150 feet long and is the biggest Texas flag in the world! Go, Texas!

7

Meet Some Famous Texans

Texans are famous for lots of different things. Some have been heroes during dangerous times. Others have played major roles in the government, serving as judges, members of Congress, and even presidents. There are also many Texans who are famous around the world as musicians, writers, and actors.

A Texas Hero

Many Texans became heroes on August 25, 2017, when Hurricane Harvey hit large parts of the state. Harvey caused the most damage of any hurricane in U.S. history. In a short time, it dumped between forty and sixty inches of rain on Houston. That's as much as the city usually has in a whole year!

At least eighty-eight people died in the hurricane.

Streets and houses flooded. People with boats rescued victims and saved them from drowning. Neighbors helped neighbors. Onlookers formed human chains to bring people across flooded streets. Stores opened to offer shelter to the homeless. Volunteers went door to door searching for anyone who needed help. For days, people worked around the clock.

This boy found his dog at a rescue
center after the hurricane.

Dr. Stephen Kimmel is a surgeon in
a suburb of Houston. His house flooded,
but when Dr. Kimmel got a call that a
boy at his hospital needed an operation,
he knew he had to help him.

Dr. Kimmel caught a ride on a rescue truck, paddled a canoe, and walked
almost a mile in waist-deep water to

get to the hospital. He made it! Because Dr. Kimmel never gave up, the boy had his operation.

It will take a long time for Texas to recover from Hurricane Harvey. But many Texans have the same spirit that Dr. Kimmel has, and they'll work hard to rebuild as soon as possible.

Government

Over the years, many famous political figures have also shown the spirit of Texas. Two presidents, Dwight D. Eisenhower and Lyndon B. Johnson, were born in Texas. Presidents George H. W. Bush and his son George W. Bush call it their home state. And Sandra Day O'Connor, the first woman on the Supreme Court, was born in El Paso and went to school there.

Willie Nelson is in the Country Music Hall of Fame.

Music

Lots of famous musicians are from Texas. In the 1970s, country-western stars from Texas, such as Willie Nelson and George Strait, began playing their music in

Austin. They helped make country-western music popular all over the world. Today, Austin is called the Live Music Capital of the World.

Popular singers Beyoncé Knowles-Carter and her sister, Solange Knowles,

Beyoncé

grew up in Houston. Beyoncé says that she is a proud Texan and that Houston is her home. She helped people who needed food after Hurricane Harvey.

Come with us and meet some more famous Texans!

Sam Houston
(1793–1863)

Sam Houston was a governor of both Tennessee and Texas. He is the only person in U.S. history ever to be governor of two states. Sam was also a lawyer, a U.S. senator, a congressman, a major general, and president of the Republic of Texas.

When Sam was a teenager, he ran away from home because he didn't want to work for his brother anymore. A Cherokee chief adopted him and renamed him the Raven.

Sam spent three years with the Cherokee, learning their language and customs. He began to love and respect them. When his life grew difficult, Sam often returned to be with the Cherokee.

Sam spoke out on the rights of the Cherokee. He once led a group of Cherokee to Washington, D.C., to meet with President Monroe. He arrived dressed in Cherokee clothing.

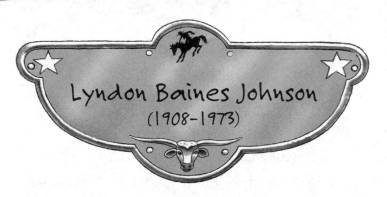

Lyndon Baines Johnson
(1908–1973)

In 1963, President John F. Kennedy was shot and killed on a visit to Dallas. Lyndon B. Johnson was his vice president. He became the thirty-sixth president of the United States.

Lyndon Johnson is famous for signing the Civil Rights Act of 1964 and the Voting Rights Act of 1965. These are the two most important civil rights laws in the history of the United States.

During President Johnson's term, America was at war with North Vietnam. As the fighting got worse, more Americans were against the war. Because of this, Johnson decided not to run for president again. He retired to his Texas ranch.

Lady Bird Johnson was Lyndon Johnson's wife and first lady of the United States. She was a good businesswoman who made speeches that helped her husband win election.

As first lady, Lady Bird helped pass laws to make America more beautiful by getting rid of billboards and litter along the highways. Lady Bird also urged people to plant flowers on their roadsides. Because bluebonnets and Indian paintbrushes grow well in Texas, she suggested that Texans plant a lot of them. Lady Bird said, "Where flowers bloom, there is hope."

Thanks to Lady Bird, drivers enjoy wildflowers along highways all over Texas. Her love of nature inspired a program against littering, with a famous bumper sticker that says "Don't mess with Texas!"

Barbara Jordan
(1936-1996)

Barbara Jordan was a teacher, lawyer, and civil rights leader. Barbara was also the first African American woman in the Texas Senate. In fact, she was the first African American man or woman in the state senate since 1883! She then became the first woman from Texas and the first African American woman from the South to serve in the U.S. House of Representatives.

The Democratic Party asked Barbara to give the most important speech at the 1976 Democratic National Convention, when Democrats choose their candidate for president. Barbara was the first African American ever to have this honor. In 1994, Barbara was awarded the Presidential Medal of Freedom.

Red Adair was a legend in Texas. He was an expert at putting out oil well fires. It's one of the most dangerous jobs anywhere! Red invented a way to put explosives in the wells to stop them from burning. After that, firefighters must cover the well. While they're doing all of this, the well might explode at any time.

Over the years, Red and his crew put out over 2,000 oil fires both on land and on oil rigs in the sea. In the Sahara Desert, they once stopped a fire that had flames shooting 450 feet into the air! In 1991, when Red was seventy-five years old, he went to Kuwait to put out fires that Iraqi soldiers had set in a large oilfield.

He once said, "I've traveled all over the world, but I don't think there is any place better than Texas."

Selena Quintanilla Pérez
(1971–1995)

Selena is known as the Queen of Tejano Music. When she was very young, Selena began singing at her father's restaurant with his band. Her brother and sister were also in the band. Selena became so popular that when she was fifteen, she was voted the best Tejano female singer of the year. In 1994, she won a Grammy for best Mexican American album.

Selena played at concerts with as many as 60,000 people in the audience. Her albums have sold more than 60 million copies.

In 1995, Selena was twenty-three years

old. She was planning to fire a woman who worked for her. The woman shot and killed Selena.

Her fans were devastated. George W. Bush, who was the governor of Texas at the time, declared her birthday Selena Day in Texas. She is remembered as one of the most important Latin musicians of all time.

8

Deep in the Heart of Texas

Today, cities in Texas are alive with business and energy. Some of the largest companies in the world have their headquarters there.

Texas has grown from 11 million people in 1970 to 28 million in 2017. On Houston's streets, you might hear people speaking over ninety different languages.

The Past Today

At one time, the Alamo had thirty buildings.

Texans are proud of their past. There are historical sites all over, from the San Jacinto Battleground to the pink Texas State Capitol building in Austin. But the most beloved site of all is the Alamo.

The fort is almost 300 years old and has over 2 million visitors a year. The city of San Antonio has plans to spend millions of dollars repairing buildings there. The United Nations honored the Alamo by naming it (and four other missions in San Antonio) a World Heritage site.

Kids Celebrating Texas!

Beginning in kindergarten, kids in Texas learn Texas history. They study the bravery of Sam Houston, Lyndon Johnson's civil rights bills, and Barbara

Jordan's struggle to serve her state and her country. Their schools celebrate Texas Independence Day in March.

During class, kids might imagine themselves rescuing people in the Galveston and Houston hurricanes or rounding up cattle on a ranch.

No matter where their families came from, Texas kids are connected to each other through their state's history. Most of them would probably agree that "Once a Texan, always a Texan!" And others might warn people not to ever mess with Texas.

Doing More Research

There's a lot more you can learn about Texas. The fun of research is seeing how many different sources you can explore.

Books

Most libraries and bookstores have books about Texas.

Here are some things to remember when you're using books for research:

1. You don't have to read the whole book. Check the table of contents and the index to find the topics you're interested in.

2. Write down the name of the book.

When you take notes, make sure you write down the name of the book in your notebook so you can find it again.

3. Never copy exactly from a book.

When you learn something new from a book, put it in your own words.

4. Make sure the book is <u>nonfiction</u>.

Some books tell make-believe stories about Texas. Make-believe stories are called *fiction*. They're fun to read, but not good for research.

Research books have facts and tell true stories. They are called *nonfiction*. A librarian or teacher can help you make sure the books you use for research are nonfiction.

Here are some good nonfiction books about Texas:

- *Leaders in the Texas Revolution: United for a Cause* by Kelly Rodgers
- *Sam Houston: A Fearless Statesman* by Joanne Mattern
- *The Story of Texas* by John Edward Weems
- *The Texas Fact and Picture Book: Fun Facts for Kids About Texas* by Gina McIntyre
- *Texas Today: Leading America into the Future* by Patrice Sherman
- *War, Cattle, and Cowboys: Texas as a Young State* by Heather E. Schwartz
- *What Was the Alamo?* by Pam Pollack and Meg Belviso

Museums

Many museums in Texas can help you learn more about the state and its history.

When you go to a museum:

1. Be sure to take your notebook!
Write down anything that catches your interest. Draw pictures, too!

2. Ask questions.
There are almost always people at museums who can help you find what you're looking for.

3. Check the calendar.
Many museums have special events and activities just for kids!

Here are some Texas museums:

- The Alamo (San Antonio)
- The Bryan Museum (Galveston)
- Bullock Texas State History Museum (Austin)
- The Hall of State (Dallas)
- National Multicultural Western Heritage Museum and Hall of Fame (Fort Worth)
- San Antonio Missions National Historical Park
- Space Center Houston
- Tejano R.O.O.T.S. Hall of Fame (Alice)

The Internet

Many websites have lots of facts about Texas. Some also have activities that can help make learning about Texas easier.

Ask your teacher or your parents to help you find more websites like these:

- american-historama.org/1829-1841
  -jacksonian-era/texas-revolution.htm
- enchantedlearning.com/usa/states/texas
- kids.nationalgeographic.com/explore
  /states/texas
- texashistory.unt.edu
- tshaonline.org/handbook
- westernexpansion.mrdonn.org
  /alamo.html

Bibliography

Brands, H. W. *Lone Star Nation: The Epic Story of the Battle for Texas Independence.* New York: Anchor Books, 2005.

Bredeson, Carmen. *The Spindletop Gusher: The Story of the Texas Oil Boom.* Houston: Bright Sky Press, 2011.

Campbell, Randolph B. *Gone to Texas: A History of the Lone Star State.* 2nd ed. New York: Oxford University Press, 2017.

Fehrenbach, T. R. *Lone Star: A History of Texas and the Texans.* Boston: Da Capo Press, 2000.

James, Marquis. *The Raven: A Biography of Sam Houston.* Austin: University of Texas Press, 1988.

Lord, Walter. *A Time to Stand.* Lincoln, NE: Bison Books, 1978.

Torget, Andrew J. *Seeds of Empire: Cotton, Slavery, and the Transformation of the Texas Borderlands, 1800–1850.* Chapel Hill: University of North Carolina Press, 2015.

Index

119

122

Have you read the adventure that matches up with this book?

You'll love finding out the facts behind the fiction in

Magic Tree House®

Magic Tree House® Merlin Missions

Magic Tree House® Super Editions

#1: World at War, 1944

Magic Tree House® Fact Trackers

Dinosaurs
Knights and Castles
Mummies and Pyramids
Pirates
Rain Forests
Space
Titanic
Twisters and Other Terrible Storms
Dolphins and Sharks
Ancient Greece and the Olympics
American Revolution
Sabertooths and the Ice Age
Pilgrims
Ancient Rome and Pompeii
Tsunamis and Other Natural Disasters
Polar Bears and the Arctic
Sea Monsters
Penguins and Antarctica
Leonardo da Vinci
Ghosts
Leprechauns and Irish Folklore
Rags and Riches: Kids in the Time of Charles Dickens
Snakes and Other Reptiles
Dog Heroes
Abraham Lincoln

Pandas and Other Endangered Species
Horse Heroes
Heroes for All Times
Soccer
Ninjas and Samurai
China: Land of the Emperor's Great Wall
Sharks and Other Predators
Vikings
Dogsledding and Extreme Sports
Dragons and Mythical Creatures
World War II
Baseball
Wild West
Texas

More Magic Tree House®

Games and Puzzles from the Tree House
Magic Tricks from the Tree House
My Magic Tree House Journal
Magic Tree House Survival Guide
Animals Games and Puzzles
Magic Tree House Incredible Fact Book